SCHIRMER'S LIBRARY
OF MUSICAL CLASSICS

Vol. 957

CH. DE BÉRIOT

Op. 57

Three Duos Concertants

For Two Violins

Revised by

FRIEDR. HERMANN

Edited and Fingered by

PHILIPP MITTELL

ISBN 978-0-7935-5134-7

G. SCHIRMER, Inc.

DISTRIBUTED BY

HAL•LEONARD®
CORPORATION

7777 W. BLUEMOUND RD. P.O. BOX 13819 MILWAUKEE, WI 53213

3 Duos Concertants

◻ Down-bow
V Up-bow

VIOLIN I

Edited and fingered by Ph. Mittell

CHARLES de BÉRIOT. Op. 57

Moderato

Adagio moderato

RONDÒ
Allegro con spirito

3 Duos Concertants

⊓ Down-bow
∨ Up-bow

Edited and fingered by Ph. Mittell

VIOLIN II

CHARLES de BÉRIOT. Op.57

20966

RONDÒ
Allegro con spirito

3. Moderato, pizz.

20968

20966

RONDÒ
Allegro

risoluto

3.

20966